The Web Ranking Manual

Tom Mitsoff

Partner, PropellerheadSEO.com

DEDICATION

I would like to dedicate this book to my wife, Angela Klein, who has been a wonderful, understanding partner for me. I spend a lot of time on this and not as much time as I should with her. She is very understanding about it, and she is going to realize the benefits of all this when we get to the point of massive profitability.

CONTENTS

ACKNOWLEDGMENTS

Brett Combs is my partner in a company called Propeller Head, which is a company that does search engine optimization work for various companies. He has taught me a lot of what I know about SEO, and I owe a lot of what I've learned to him. He has been a mentor to me in this endeavor.

1 WHY SEO IS SO IMPORTANT

It is so important for people to have high rankings in Google because these days, in our current society, that is the equivalent of what a full page Yellow Pages ad used to be.

Years ago, people who wanted to get high exposure in their community for their business would just place a large Yellow Pages ad. These days, Google has replaced that as the way people find information.

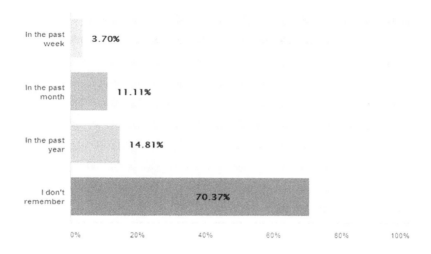

When was the most recent occasion you used the Yellow Pages?

"The last time I used a Yellow Pages was at my grandmother's house," wrote Malena Ogles of Atlanta, Georgia. "She did not have a computer."

The data and responses above were gathered in an unscientific polling of friends on my Facebook pages and my e-mail list. They served to verify and clearly confirm the premise of this book.

High organic rankings in Google are the equivalent of what a full-page Yellow Pages ad used to be, in terms of exposure and advertising. Organic means search rankings that you don't pay Google for. On Google, Bing and Yahoo, you see the paid ads at the top of the page and at the sides, and they sometimes have a slightly tinted background so you can tell that they're paid ads. The listings that come up without the shading throughout the center of the search results page are ones for which people have not made a payment to Google for positioning. Rather, their position is based on Google's proprietary algorithm which ranks web pages to determine their potential value to people searching for information.

Twenty or 30 years ago and more, when people wanted to find out the solution to some problem or issue they had around their house or in the community, they would go to the Yellow Pages. That is where you would find a plumber, a roofer or find any kind of specialist who could help.

Now, when was the last time YOU actually picked up the Yellow Pages? For me, it's probably been many, many years, literally.

(Case in point: As I was editing this chapter, my wife called out to me from the front porch of our single-family home, and as I went to see what she needed, I noticed she had picked up and thrown a plastic yellow bag with what appeared to be the latest Yellow Pages just inside the front door. Three days later, guess where that book still is:)

(That book is eventually going to go straight to our recycling bin, and I suspect the same is the case for most other people.) In the afore-mentioned unscientific survey, I asked:

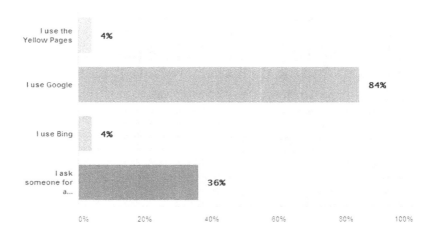

When you need to find a service provider in your neighborhood or town, how do you find one?

(The full text of the option which people selected 36 percent of the time was "I ask someone for a recommendation." All of which goes to show that word of mouth certainly is not dead.)

Internet marketer and Daytona Beach, Fla., resident Chad Cook, a colleague of mine, summed it up: "Only time Yellow Pages is ever used is putting a dot com after it. Everything I do is online."

Lauren Fink of Quantico, Virginia reminded that printed books cannot respond as well as trusted friends.

"Another reason I don't use yellow pages is because I find better recommendations online," she wrote in her survey response. "My favorite way lately, is to use my moms-only Facebook groups to find recommendations from other moms about service providers. The two in my area here in Virginia are Ready, Set, Sell Stafford and Mommy Traders - both are like local, mom-only Craigslists but are useful for asking questions. My latest was 'Please recommend a good jeweler,' and I received 14 comments within a few hours."

Everyone now goes to Google or to one of the search engines to find the things they want to find. Recent studies show that more than 80 percent of people go on search engines before they make a purchase. They want to compare shops; they want to do research on what it is that they need to buy or the service they need. Having a high spot in search engines makes it easier for people to find you – like having a full-page Yellow Pages ad next to a liner or small rectangle ad for your competitor. The full-page ad will always get more attention.

It just makes sense, and there are statistics to back this up, that the higher you are in the search, the more chance that you have of being clicked on and looked at. So, that's the whole objective -- to try to be as high as you can, to be as visible as you can.

It just makes basic sense. Most people will look at the front page of the search results and won't really go past that, and that's just human nature.

When you've done a search and come up with about 10 different options, for most people that is more than enough options to do comparisons and make a decision.

And the higher you are, the better. Studies show that if you're number one, you'll get about 40 percent of the clicks that are made on that search results page. If you're number two, you'll get about 20 percent. If you're number three, you'll get about 10 percent, and then the rest of the seven results left on that first page get the rest of those clicks. So, when you're number 10, for example, you might get about 1 percent or 2 percent as opposed to the 40 percent of the number one on that page. More than anything else, that explains why there is so much emphasis in people's minds on "how do I get to number one," because you get 40 times more clicks than you would if you're in the number 10 position on the first page. It also explains why the organic search engine optimization initiative in business has become such a big business.

When you have a high organic ranking and someone clicks on your link, you don't pay for that click. If you're an AdWords advertiser (someone who pays for those slightly-shaded placements at the top and sides of pages that we mentioned previously), you pay every time somebody clicks on your link. Depending on what kind of business you're in, those clicks can be very, very expensive.

If you're a good businessperson, you have done the math and figured out that if you are going to pay $4 per click, you know what your return on that is going to be and whether or not you can make it work profitably. In almost every case, organic search engine optimization is the best way to go to get the best bang for your buck. You'll pay someone to do the up-front work, but you're not paying for each click. In Yellow Pages terms, it would be like being charged every time someone calls you on the phone.

Most readers of this book know what SEO is, but if you don't, it is the abbreviation for "search engine optimization." SEO is the process of configuring your website so that it is viewed favorably by Google and the other search engines and, therefore, receives as high of a ranking in the search engines as possible. It's what we're all going to be talking about here throughout this book.

Organic SEO would be oh-so-simple if Google would just tell everyone the best ways to do it. But the truth is that no one knows 100 percent for sure, because Google has never actually published its ranking algorithm.

Google has not published a guide because they do not want people to know how to manipulate the search results. They want the consumers who use Google to believe that the rankings they're seeing are completely unbiased and unaffected by anything other than a very specific standard that Google applies to everybody.

However, there are many SEO specialists who have reverse-engineered the Google ranking process to find out what qualities and attributes make one site or page rank higher than another organically. Through this reverse engineering process, there is a very good understanding of what's important in Google's eyes and what isn't, even though Google does not publish it. We've learned what it is that they look for, and this book will reveal it to you.

Google actually views SEO in an unfavorable light. They believe if someone is trying to search-optimize his or her site, he or she is trying to falsely improve its position in the rankings. So, it's considered a manipulation of Google's product and they don't like it. Part of what we will cover in this book is the importance of making your SEO efforts look natural – as though it is the result of genuine outside user action, reaction and behavior, and not a contrived campaign.

Google has its systems programmed to detect sites which appear to be getting unnatural SEO attention.

They have, in their massive computer system, signals that go off and say, in effect, "Uh-oh, someone is really trying too hard to make this site higher than it should be, and as a result, we're going to penalize them and drop them even further than they were to begin with." (Or something like that.) ☺

Part of the difficulty of an SEO practice is to try to make sure that, while you're optimizing it for the best possible result within Google's tolerance level, you don't overdo it. If you overdo it and Google detects it, then you're basically sunk. You've basically killed your site for any hope ever, ever being ranked in Google. So, it's a very delicate balance.

If Google penalizes you and your site drops into the dark pit of the internet, nobody will ever find you again online. And if people can't find you, they can't buy your products and services.

Despite all of Google's best efforts to provide quality search results to its users, sometimes you'll do a search and one of the top sites that comes up is one that looks spammy, garish and amateurish. Most people are surprised to learn that the artistic look and layout of the website is not at all considered by Google. The Big G not look at a site and say, "Well, that's prettier. Well, that is a nice design or that's a nice image." They do not consider that whatsoever.

What they consider -- we'll talk about more later on the specifics -- has to do with the text that's on the page and the links and coding of the images that are on the page. So, you can have a website that basically has almost no content at all show up near the top. More often than not, that's because somebody has consciously optimized that site to rank highly.

Once the site is ranked highly, then the owner or manager can then add content to turn the site into a profitable business. In what most people would see as a counter-intuitive work plan, the owner-manager will work on the parts of the website that humans look at AFTER making sure the often-invisible-to-human-eyes components that Google's bots love are in place.

When a website builder is striving for high rankings, he or she is building to be seen by Google's computers, not human eyes. Surprisingly to most, there is a highly divergent perception of what makes a quality page between the two.

This is the approach we use, and it is a great way to see if you can get ranked before you spend a lot of time and resources on creating specific sales content. We haven't addressed Bing and Yahoo much here, and there is a reason for that. This is my opinion only, based on personal experience, but Yahoo and Bing are insignificant, compared to Google.

According to the respected website SearchEngineWatch.com, Google had about 66 percent of all Internet searches done in April 2013. Bing had about 17 percent, and Yahoo had about 13 percent. Google's market share is down from its highest point a few years back, but not down significantly enough to signal a major shift in online searching behavior and habits. As I'm working for my clients, I frankly don't worry about Yahoo and Bing. I don't spend time trying to optimize for Yahoo or Bing because you're talking about, in either case, about maybe 12 to 13 percent of the people who are doing searches anywhere who are actually using those two.

I would much rather optimize for a search engine where two-thirds of the people who are doing searches are. Bing and Yahoo's organic ranking algorithms are not the same as Google's, and for the reasons mentioned above, there has not been as much research and reverse engineering done on the former two. In mid-2013, as it has been for quite awhile, getting a top ranking in Bing or Yahoo is kind of like kissing your sister, to use an old cliché. So what? You'll never achieve the level of success that you can with a similar ranking in Google. (Having said all of that, however, we have found that high rankings in Bing and Yahoo very often occur as an unintended consequence of the SEO work done for Google.)

For verification, here is what the people who responded to my survey said about their search engine use:

How often do you use Google?

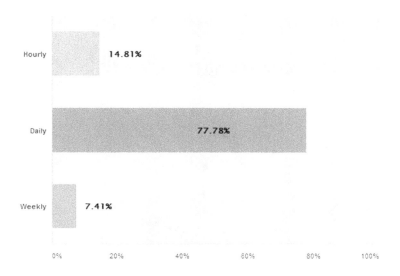

Internet marketer Gary Chappelle of Duluth, Georgia confirmed my suspicions in his response:

"I am so used to using Google now that I rarely use any offline method of finding a service provider in my area. It's just second nature now. I'm not sure what I'd do if the Internet ever disappeared."

On the other hand:

How often do you use Yahoo?

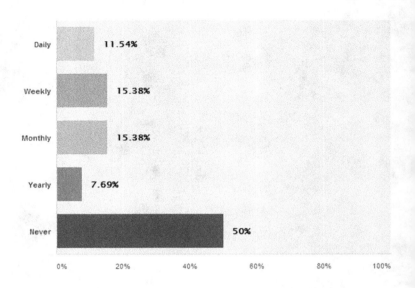

How often to you use Bing?

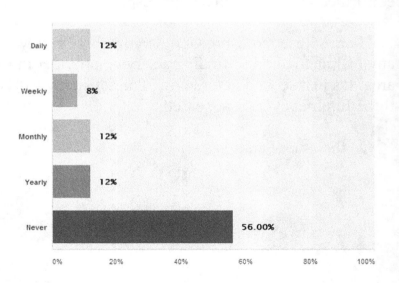

There are many important facets to a successful SEO campaign, but the most important part without question is keyword research. It is critical to know what people are searching for on the Internet and to be able to put your website in a top position for those searches. One mistake that some people make is they will try to get (or stumble into) number one ranking for a term like "Monkeys that can mimic Texas search engine optimization practitioners' habits." While you can easily do that, it doesn't matter because nobody will ever search for it. So, you have to, as you're putting a plan together, understand that finding out what people are searching for in Google is the most important thing. And understand that being number one for a search term that nobody searches for is nothing more than a moral victory.

A great example is one of our top clients who was starting a national business from scratch, and he wanted to be found in Google.

When I first talked to him, I asked what business he wanted to be in. He said he wanted to be in the water park or water slide repair business. I did keyword research with the Google Keyword Planner (formerly and better known as the Google Keyword Tool) and typed in water slide, just to see what related terms people are searching for.

The term that is searched most often by people who are looking for that service is "water slide repair," so that is the keyword term that I focused upon. We've got him on the first page for that term, and many, many other related search terms. He's getting lots and lots of business based on not just a main keyword search, but several others.

All successful SEO campaigns consist of "on-page" and "off-page" factors. On-page SEO means changes you make to your actual website. Off-page SEO consists of actions that are taken not on your actual site, and we'll talk more about that later. These are two very, very distinct processes you go through to increase your site's ranking. There's a very important aspect of it that has nothing to do with the page or site that you control.

Have you ever heard someone say, or seen someone advertise, that he or she can guarantee you a number one spot in Google? Sounds great, but that is absolutely impossible to promise -- because you do not control Google.

Also, there are millions of other people in the world who are trying to do the same thing -- getting a keyword optimized or a website optimized for a specific keyword search. And all you can control is what happens on your own site. You cannot directly control what happens on someone else's site. So, it's very possible that someone else has a better plan, a better strategy, a more effective strategy than you do to get rankings.

Therefore, you should steer clear of anyone who promises a number one ranking. And, if you are an aspiring SEO service provider, you should never promise that.

However, you can build higher payments for achieving higher rankings into your fee structure. Most people don't mind paying extra for premium service and results.

If you're in business and don't employ organic SEO, you're basically just hoping that what you have on your website is going to be good enough, and I would say 99 percent of the people really don't know what the critical components are. Fortunately for you, now that you are reading this manual, you will be in the select company of the 1 percent who do know.

If you're not going to try to use organic SEO, you basically will be out of luck. The odds will be infinitesimally against you being able to get the rankings you need by chance.

Google is always changing. It changes all the time, and that's part of the difficulty. If you're not in on the information loop, knowing where to find the information about changes they're making, then you really can just get left behind. That's just part of the difficulty of someone who is not a professional at this to be able to do it and do it well.

CHAPTER RECAP

If you want to be found by your customers these days, you don't do it with Yellow Pages; you do it with search engines. And you can either do it through paid ads on Google AdWords, or you can do it through organic search engine optimization. When people click on you, you don't pay for those clicks, and that can be, in the long term, much, much less expensive, in fact, free in a lot of ways as opposed to the AdWords.

2 EVERY SEO PLAN NEEDS A SOLID FOUNDATION

If you're constructing a house or a commercial building, you're not going to get the results you want if you just show up at the site with a bunch of tools and lumber and try to wing it.

You may get started quickly if you know how to use a hammer and power saw, but as you get further along in the process, things are going to go a little haywire. You need a blueprint to build a house or a skyscraper correctly, and it's the same way in SEO. You need a blueprint before you start of what specifically you're going to do and what specific results you want to achieve. As in construction, you can really go awry if you don't have a plan.

As part of any solid SEO plan blueprint, the first question we would ask a potential client is, "What exactly do you want to promote?" They may have a website already that they like. Or, they may not have a site. In that case, we would make some recommendations on what kind of website to build.

The next question is should the client use his or her existing website, or start a new one? We would look at the existing website and do a critical analysis of what the client has in place. We would use our knowledge of the Google ranking factors, what works and what doesn't work, and make a recommendation.

For the best chance of ranking success -- unless you've done a lot of things right before contacting us – we often will recommend starting from scratch with a new website, incorporating the elements we're going to lay out here. Once a website has been built in a way that Google does not necessarily like, it's very tough to reverse that.

For example: A potential client manages an apartment complex and he wants to do the best online promotion possible. We're going to analyze what we need to do, including researching what search terms people are entering in Google to find apartments for rent in town.

Then, we would look at the client's existing website and say, "OK, is this something that's going to help or hinder you in trying to get that done, based on what we know about what Google considers to be a good website ranking in that search?"

The next step -- which we mentioned in the first chapter --- is keyword research. We would do the research in the Google Keyword Planner to find out what people are typing into Google to find apartments in -- let's just say we're in Beavercreek, Ohio. We'd look up Beavercreek Ohio apartments in the Google Keyword Planner to find out what are the most frequent phrases people actually type into Google when they are seeking information about Beavercreek Ohio apartments. Like any other promotion or advertising initiative, we're trying to get the most people to your offer.

IMPORTANT NOTE: When you do this search, if you are focusing on a specific community or town, you need to use the "Include/Exclude" tool in the left column on the Keyword Planner page. Where it says, "Only include keywords containing the following terms," enter the name of the town, without the state. This will save you the problem of having to muddle through a bunch of results that are useless to you because they relate to apartment searches on a global instead of local level.

The results of this exercise help to illustrate the value of keyword research:

"Beavercreek Ohio apartments," the term we typed in, gets 140 monthly searches, according to Google. However …

"Apartments in Beavercreek Ohio" gets 590 searches per month! By doing keyword research, we have already found a term that people search for 350 times per month MORE than the term we ASSUMED would be the most frequently typed-in phrase.

The most important point: ALWAYS do the research.

NEVER assume.

A big step up on the search engine optimization difficulty ladder would be Los Angeles, California, a very, very large city.

We typed "Los Angeles apartments" into the Keyword Planner, and found:

"Apartments in Los Angeles" gets 6,600 monthly searches;

"Los Angeles apartments" (as well as "Apartments for rent in Los Angeles") gets 5,400 monthly searches.

So by doing the research, we discovered a term that gets 1,200 more monthly searches than the one we initially identified.

The Google Keyword Planner can be used by anybody. Actually, it's free, and the way you find it is you go on the Internet and do a search for Google Keyword Planner. What you'll find is that you have to have a Google account, which most people do. You may be asked to enter a credit card number, but that is only because Google wants to have your card number on file in hopes that you will one day have the need to place AdWords ads. You will not be charged to use the keyword planner tool.

Let's say a client's apartment complex is called Sensational Living Suites. That owner/manager might be thinking to himself, "I want to be number one when people search for Sensational Living Suites." We would say, "Yes, you do. but …"

Would the average person in Beavercreek looking for an apartment really type in a search for "Sensational Living Suites," or would they search for "Beavercreek Ohio apartments" or "apartments in Beavercreek Ohio?" Unless your business has widespread name recognition, most people searching online are not going to type the name of your apartment complex in when searching for apartments.

That's why we use the Google Keyword Planner: type the term you THINK might be the most-searched one in your niche, hit go, and then get a listing of how many times each of the similar terms are searched in Google in an average month. Anyone can do it, and I would encourage people to try it so they understand this valuable free tool.

Remember that just because the number of monthly searches a term gets seems small, it is not necessarily a bad keyword to target. In a local search, such as one for Beavercreek, Ohio, it can be very targeted and important. It may not be important to somebody in Spain or Russia, but those people are very unlikely to be looking to spend money on apartments in Beavercreek, Ohio, anyway.

When you're talking about tens of thousands or hundreds of thousands of monthly searches on a specific term, you most often will see numbers like that in searches that aren't focused on a geographic region.

WHAT INFRASTRUCTURE DO I NEED?

If you're going to do a full-scale search engine optimization program, you have to have a financial budget. It's not free, even if you're doing it yourself.

You will need to budget for:
External website hosting
Purchasing and renewing domain names
Linkbuilding software, such as SENuke
Virtual Private Server (VPS) to run SENuke
Purchasing high page-rank backlinks (more on that later)
Other miscellaneous costs associated with SENuke
Monthly membership for MajesticSEO.com

WHAT IS AN SEO "SILO"?

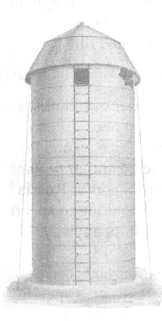

This is something that not many people know about, but it is one of the keys to this entire process.

Everyone knows what an actual silo is. It's a tall cylindrical structure used in farming to store grain. If you pour a bucket of water into the top of that full silo, the water will trickle down in and around all of the grain until most of the water reaches the bottom.

In an SEO silo, we want "link juice" to trickle down the contents of the silo to have a positive ranking effect on all of the pages it touches. (More on what "link juice" is later.)

A website can have an unlimited number of silos, and they will all fall below the website's home page. For this example, let's imagine that we have a price comparison website, bestprices.com. (NOTE: That domain is already taken and in use. This example is for illustration purposes only.)

What we're going to do is we want to build a "silo" below that home page. Using our barnyard silo analogy, the home page, with a primary keyword of "best prices," is above the silo. We're placing it above the silos, because in our SEO plan, there may be several silos if we have several keywords we are trying to rank:

Best prices

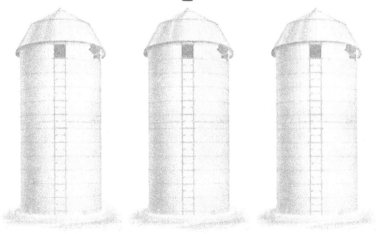

Using the Google Keyword planner, you're going to look for a term that's related to best prices that is not quite as competitive. When we say not quite as competitive, that's another way of saying fewer monthly searches. Generally speaking, the fewer the number of searches a keyword term gets, the fewer people are trying to optimize for it.

We have "best prices" with 4,400 searches per month, according to Google. Inside our silo at the top will be another term that we're targeting that is a subset of "best prices." This means that the Google Keyword Planner considers the term related to "best prices." Using the Planner, we found one with 1,600 monthly searches, "best hotel prices."

Best prices

Best hotel
prices

In effect, "best hotel prices" is a subset of the homepage keyword. It's best prices not of everything, but just on hotels. And then, below that, you want something that is even more granular regarding hotels: "Best prices on Vegas hotels" gets 10 searches per month.

Best prices

Best hotel prices

Best prices on Vegas hotels

So, as we're going down the silo, we are getting more and more specific on the term. The first term at the top best prices was very wide and very expansive and, as we're going down in the silo, we have "best hotel prices" -- a little bit more specific; then "best prices on Vegas hotels," even more specific. Then, I'm going to do one more search, and I found that an even more granular term – "best prices on luxury hotels in Las Vegas" – gets so few searches that Google doesn't report them.

(In a campaign for a client, we would never target a term that gets zero searches. This example is for illustrative purposes only.)

Best prices

Best hotel
prices

Best prices
on Vegas
hotels

Best prices on
luxury hotels in
Las Vegas

So, what we have done has created a silo that would appear, if you're looking at it in terms of the number of searches on each one of those terms, it would look like a funnel. It would be much wider at the top and, as you go down toward the bottom, it's much more narrow. Each one of the terms in the silo is going to be the title of a page on your site.

Your home page would be "best prices," and then you'll have pages titled "best hotel prices," "best prices on Vegas hotels," and "best prices on luxury hotels in Las Vegas." We are going to create a hyperlink chain within these pages, and the fact that they have such similar names is one of the keys that Google likes.

Google's "bots" that automatically roam the Internet and find new web pages will say (metaphorically), "This is really a focused website." Google's algorithms will perceive the site (and silo) as well-thought out and well-designed, due to the closely related names of these interlinked pages. To human eyes, it may or may not be, depending on what content we put on it ultimately. What we're doing at this point is making the site attractive to Google's bots and internal algorithms.

Next, we interlink the silo in a very specific way. The top page inside the silo, "best hotel prices," links down to "best prices on Vegas hotels." That page, in turn, gets linked down to "best prices on luxury hotels in Las Vegas." The page at the bottom of the silo then links up to "best prices," the homepage which is outside the silo.

Later in this process, you're going to create or purchase links from pages with high Google "page rank" to the top page inside the silo. The "link juice" -- benefits that a page's ranking receives in Google's eyes because it has a link from a page with high "page rank" -- will flow throughout the silo and even to the site's home page due to the links you have created.

Google assigns a "page rank" (or, "PR") between zero (low end) and 10 (highest) to every page it indexes. Most pages are ranked zero and 1. Links from pages ranked zero have, not surprisingly, zero benefit to the recipient page. Links from PR 1 pages have negligible impact.

Links from pages that are PR 2 and 3 say to Google, the site being linked to must be a good site. After all, if a site we rank at PR 2 or 3 is linking to it, there must be quality on the linked site.

If you get a link from a page that is a page ranked 4 through 10, those are very rare. In Google's eyes, those are the absolute best pages that they have in their index. If those pages are linking to you, that means your site must be outstanding. Links from sites with high PR are shown to result in substantial positive changes in organic search engine rankings.

So, we're going to find external pages that have high page rank and create links from them back to our own site. It is commonly known in the SEO community that as you go up the PR scale, the "link juice" benefits increase geometrically.

In simple terms, a PR 5 is not just a little bit better than a PR 4, but its increased benefits in Google's eyes are staggering. Similarly, a PR 6 has staggeringly more benefit than a PR 5, and that pattern continues up the PR ladder.

Pages with very high PR are Internet royalty in Google's eyes. If we find an external page that let's just say a PR 5, and we are able to create a link from that PR 5 page to the top page inside our silo, there is so much good ranking karma and benefit from that PR 5 that it spills down to the pages below it in the silo – as long as they are hyperlinked.

Some of that "link juice" trickles all the way down to the bottom page in the silo. And because that bottom page in the silo is linked to the home page, some "link juice" cycles back to the homepage. So that one link from a PR page affects not only one page on your site, but many pages. There's an accumulation effect.

Instead of having to build maybe five links from outside sources, you can build one really good one and get a lot of the same benefits. And that can save you both time and money in some cases. We'll discuss link-building in much more detail later.

If you have done all of the recommended on-page optimization, but you're still ranking behind other competitors, the next step is to investigate your competitors' backlink profiles.

In other words, how many backlinks they have, and from what Google PR's they originate.

MajesticSEO.com is going to become part of your

SEO online library if you plan to do any effective work. You can go there and put in the URL of any website like your own, and Majestic SEO will tell you is how many links are coming into your site from other websites around the entire Internet. And, you can do the same for your competitors to learn how their backlink profile differs from yours.

In effect, it gives you a roadmap to follow to be able to match or exceed your competitors' backlink profiles. And, it can tell you in some cases that no matter how much you do, you face an uphill battle with no guarantee of success. In this way, Majestic SEO can help save you time you might otherwise spend waging an unwinnable rankings war.

It's a free membership for the basic Majestic SEO service, which is what I usually use. There's a higher end paid service that you'll need if you want to get into doing campaigns that are national or worldwide in scope.

We know that one of the absolute keys to success is getting external sites to link to you. Which begs the question: How in the heck do I do that?

There's are a lot of answers to this question and a lot of ways to do it. The slowest way and the least effective way is for a human to send messages to other website owners asking them to trade backlinks. That was popular maybe seven to 10 years ago, but these days, it's too slow.

The number of links you need back to have a good

ranking for a competitive term is so high that you just can't do it manually. Sites like Facebook have literally BILLIONS of backlinks coming to it. So, you would never try to beat Facebook on anything really competitive because there's almost no chance.

Why are backlinks so important? In Google's eyes, they are, in effect, votes. In very basic terms, you link to things you like. Facebook users post links all the time, in effect telling the world what they want to share. The more backlinks to your site, the more people think it has worthy content, from Google's perspective.

There is software that can create backlinks automatically for you. It finds sites with high PR and does the work for you.

SEO Nuke is software that I use to create massive backlink campaigns. It's a little expensive, about $160 per month. You'd have to really be into SEO and know that you're going to make some money monthly as a result to cover this cost. SEO Nuke will reach out into the web and create hundreds or even thousands of links back to your site in the correct format that Google likes, all automatically.

It takes about 30 minutes to set up a campaign, and you set it to run for over a period of weeks. You do that so that it doesn't appear to Google's bots that all of the links are coming at the same time. That would look very weird if your site had no links, and all of a sudden, it had a thousand. That would not seem naturally occurring. The software can be configured so that these thousand links are created gradually over the time period you specify, up to 30 days. I use it,. and it works great.

It all points back to the keyword research and that knowing what keywords are the ones upon which to focus. Once you have mastered keyword research and you can build backlinks to pages optimized for your chosen keywords, SEONuke works great.

CAN YOU SEO AFFILIATE LINKS?

Most readers of this book have seen offers on the Internet where you can promote someone else's product and make a commission on any sales that result. Amazon.com is a great example of that.

You can actually sign up with Amazon as an affiliate, and if your link that you put out to people about a certain product or a book ends up resulting in a sale, you get a commission from Amazon. Affiliate links include unique code for each individual affiliate. Amazon and other companies track affiliate links. They know when they make a sale that originated from an affiliate's link.

You're not selling something that you yourself own or that you yourself have made. You're selling someone else's product, and therefore you're getting a small commission off of a product that someone else owns or controls.

Getting affiliate links ranked is a strategy that has been tried over and over. Why? What if you were able to get YOUR Amazon affiliate link for "Fifty Shades of

Gray" ranked number one in the search for that book title? You would make a lot of money, probably millions of dollars. But no one has been able to do that consistently and successfully. Google knows what affiliate links look like and how they're constructed. Google knows if they allow affiliate links to be successfully optimized, all Google searches would be filled with nothing but individuals' affiliate links at the top of results. Google does not want the search engine to become basically a free-for-all for people trying to sell affiliate products.

So the strategy that successful affiliates use is to create their own sites on domains they purchase, and then have their affiliate links within the content they create on the site's pages. It's not as good as a direct affiliate link ranked in the top three of Google, but it's the next best thing.

WHAT IS BLACK HAT SEO?

There are different ways to accomplish these tasks we have described, like backlinking. SEO Nuke is definitely a good way to do it, but there are other ways which are considered "Black Hat," or not very ethical. They're out there, and they often cost less. The down side is that if you use these methods that are not on the up and up, they will get you penalized like you won't believe. They will often work quicker than the usual methods, but they will get you penalized much, much worse and deeper.

A rather noteworthy case of this occurred in 2011, when the New York Times discovered that

JCPenney.com ranked very highly in organic SEO results for almost every product they sold. It turned out that the source of that was an extensive (and frankly, not well-enough-disguised) campaign to buy links from high PR sites back to JCPenney.com's product pages.

As mentioned previously, Google does not like to have its product manipulated, and when the New York Times presented what it had learned to Google, the big G acted quickly to "slap" JCPenney's rankings out of prominent positions.

So you have a decision if you want something to rank very, very quickly. You can use methods that are kind of off the beaten path and maybe not so ethical, but when you're discovered, your site or link is gone for good. It's a decision to make, and our decision is not to describe those options here.

On the other hand, you'll hear the term "White Hat SEO," which is the methods that do not get you in trouble as long as you're doing them correctly.

If you're talking to somebody and you find out that maybe they're using Black Hat methods, you probably want to stay clear of them.

Make sure you're aware that there are good guys and bad guys, and you want to stay away from the bad guys.

If you're not sure, you can always do some research on an individual or company to learn more.

CHAPTER REVIEW

Before you start, understand what your SEO plan is, what your goal is and what are you going to do to get there. What tools are you going to use to get there?

It's just like the building analogy. If you're going in without the tools, without the blueprint, without the lumber, your structure is not going to be very good. When you're competing with the world and millions of others in many cases, you need to bring a solid blueprint and your best tool set to have a chance.

3 HOW TO GET THE DOMAIN NAME YOU NEED FOR SEO SUCCESS

Most everyone reading this book knows how to purchase a domain name from one of the many companies that broker that service. What we want to cover here is how to find out what domain name gives you the best chance for SEO success, as well as how to grab effective variations of it that you may not have considered.

One of the most important factors in getting ranked highly is called "exact match domain," or EMD. It means, from Google's perspective, that your domain name exactly matches the search term typed in by the search engine user.

We used earlier the example of Apartments in Los Angeles. If we can find and purchase Apartments in Los Angeles as an available domain name, we will have such a great chance of getting that website ranked highly for that term, you wouldn't believe it.

There's probably nothing more important in being able to get a site ranked highly.

As I edited this book, I did this search on GoDaddy on August 18, 2013, and learned that apartmentsinlosangeles.com is not available -- which actually played right into the plan for this chapter. More often than not, you're not going to get a .com for a competitive keyword term.

This is where a lot of people just throw up their hands and walk away, but this is where SEO practitioners roll up their sleeves and go to work. Research by numerous professionals has shown that after .com, the next suffix most likely to rank, all other factors being equal, is a .org. So we'll then check to see if the domain name apartmentsinlosangeles.org is available.

Nope. But we're not done yet. For the purposes of ranking, the only suffixes I will touch are .com and .org. In a rare circumstance in which there is not much competition, I may go for a .net. There are many other suffixes out there such as .us, .tv, .me, .ws, .co, and on and on. Hundreds more are coming soon, but they are basically useless for the purposes of getting ranked. If you're not worried about ranking, then any of those domain suffixes are fine.

The .net is also gone for apartmentsinlosangeles, but that actually is not what I would have checked next after the .org. The next check is hyphenated .com and .org domains.

Ninety-nine percent of the time domain names consist of letters of multiple words running together with no spaces in between them -- so it looks like one long word, even though it isn't. There's one way around this.

With the .com, .org and .net EMDs all gone, the next step in the domain name search is to put a hyphen in between each word. So instead of apartmentsinlosangeles, I'm searching domain name brokers to see if apartments-in-los-angeles is available. And voila! On August 18, 2013, that hyphenated domain was available as .com, .org and .net! (As an SEO practitioner, or someone who wants to build a business around that keyword and domain, you would grab apartments-in-los-angeles.com if available, and if not, then the .org. The ranking power of the .net drops off substantially.)

It may look a little unusual, but understand the method behind the madness. Google reads dashes in a URL as spaces. So when you type in "apartments in Los Angeles" in a Google search, Google indexes the hyphenated version as an exact-match domain (EMD), with every bit as much ranking power as the unhyphenated version.

Google has a ranking internally for how they view the value of domain suffixes. Let's just say that we have apartments-in-los-angeles.com, the same thing .net, the same thing .org. In that case, the .com is always going to be on top if everything else is equal. The .com is universally seen as the most credible domain. But surprisingly, the next one that you can get almost as good of ranking with is .org. Now you hear a lot of people that have websites with the .net at the end, but actually the best one other than if you can't get .com for your keyword, is to to go to .org. If you can get that, you are in great shape. A lot of people use .orgs to get great, great rankings with exact match domains. If I can't find an EMD in those two, then I know that my chances of high ranking are quite a bit lower if I go to the .net or the .info or something like that.

Buying a domain name is just the first step, though, in having a website. You also have to set up website hosting. Most times, you can do that with the same company from which you bought your domain name. It is important to know that just buying a domain name is not all that's required.

Once you get website hosting set up, you'll need to go to where you have stored your domain name (probably on the site where you purchased it), and change the nameservers.

You most likely will have received an e-mail or some sort of notification from the company you purchased website hosting from that the hosting is set up and live. That notice will likely include the names of your new nameservers: the new Internet servers where your website resides.

If you have your domain and website hosting with the same company, this process takes fewer steps. If you don't, let's use an example of what you'll need to do.

You've just set up hosting on for your website on Brand Y, but the domain name I bought was through Brand X. So if my domain name is sitting on Brand X and my hosting is on Brand Y, there is no natural or spontaneous connection between them, and there is no way for those two to work together unless I take some action to link them.

So I have to go to Brand X to my domain name and under where it says name servers, I'd have to enter the names of the servers that Brand Y gave to me. That's the only way that you can get the two to be linked together so that they work together and your website shows up online.

Once your site is live, you can start putting content on it. The most common application people use to do this is WordPress. About 50 percent of all websites are on WordPress. It started as a blogging platform, but now it has evolved into probably the easiest way to set up a website that's ready to go. You don't have to know a whole lot of coding, and you don't have to know a whole lot of technical stuff to do it. You can get it set up and it is just basically the easiest application to be able to add content to your website.

Most website hosting services will give you access to the back office of the website, which is where you can have WordPress (and many other applications, for that matter) installed on your site. It's easier to install WordPress through these automated methods, but I've heard numerous reports that WordPress installations done this way are much more vulnerable to hacking. I don't have the latest facts on that, so I would encourage you to do some investigation for yourself.

There is a way to manually install WordPress which is considered more hack-proof, but you really have to know your way around databases, etc., which I do not. So I go with the back-office services like Fantastico that automate the installation.

You're not required to use WordPress. It's just one of the many different applications and coding methods you can use to set up a site. But Word Press has developed as the easiest one for the most people to use. It used to be that you had to be able to know how to write the entire page in code -- not just the text that you see on the page in your browser, but all the stuff telling the servers what to do. WordPress does most of that for you. All you have to do is type in your text and put in your pictures, put it in your videos, then hit save and it shows up.

CHAPTER REVIEW

After you've done your keyword research, if you can get the exact match domain name (EMD) for that keyword in a .com or a .org you are on your way. You're not guaranteed success, but you have just put yourself in a much better position than anybody else. You should always, always do that if you can.

4 ON-PAGE MUSTS FOR SEO SUCCESS

We covered earlier the difference between on-page and off-page SEO. In this chapter, we're going to cover the things you CAN control that give you the best chance for SEO success. There is no reason not to take all of these steps if you are serious about getting your website ranked highly in Google.

First of all, **use WordPress**. Google seems to like WordPress. There have been no specific studies on this, but I think the fact that 50% of the websites out there are on WordPress just makes it obvious that a lot of them are going to be ranked in Google. The common wisdom is that Google likes WordPress. But there are plenty of websites that are not done in WordPress that rank well. For me, Word Press is easy and I just start with that.

If you have a Google account, and most people do, you can sign up for a **Google Analytics** tracking code which you put on your website. It lets you see how many visitors that you are getting to your website -- not just how many hits and how many visitors, but how they got there. Did they get there through a Google search, a Yahoo search or Bing? If they did, what keywords did they search to let them find you?

This is all very, very important to know so you can make decisions on what you're doing with SEO -- is it working? Is it not working? You can also discover statistics that jump out at you that you didn't even consider. It's a great way to give you some insight on how to improve what you see.

In any business, you have to understand what's happening to be able to make good decisions. If you don't have any analytics and you don't know how people are getting there or how many people are there, you really can't make informed decisions on what changes you might need to make.

Even if you don't have a full article on your page, you need to have a headline or title. People who are familiar with coding and blogs will know what an H1 tag is. You need to have a **headline on your page with an H1 tag** around it. That headline should include the keyword for which you are trying to optimize the page. It HAS to have your keyword in it if you want to have success.

You need to have a **YouTube video** on the page. YouTube is held in high regard by Google – in no small part because Google owns YouTube. So it's not surprising that they would see inclusion of a YouTube video as a real positive thing.

You need to have two specific links on the page: one

to an "authority website" (and we'll talk more about what that is later), and a link to another page on your own website and that is part of the silo that we outlined in Chapter 2.

You must have a **title tag with your main keyword in the tag**. In WordPress, you can make sure you have this set up by going to the Settings > General screen in the administrative dashboard and entering the title in the field indicated for it. (There's also a field for a subtitle, which is not as critical.)

In basic HTML coding, there's a bracket that looks like this: <title>Your site title here</title>. You see what's between the brackets of the title tag at the very top of your browser window. There is a very thin blue or black bar that tells you what the website is about. That is what Google sees as the title of your website. That absolutely has to have your keyword in it for you to have a chance to rank highly in competitive situations. It used to be that the title tag was absolutely the most important thing that you needed to do. Now because so many people have learned that and are doing it, the exact match domain is becoming more important.

Still, if you don't have your keyword in your title tag, then you might as well just stop. What's inside the title tag not only shows up at the top of your browser window, it's what shows up to identify your website in Google search results.

For example, do a Google search for the word Google. At the top of the results when I did the search was a hyperlink for "Google ad words-online advertising by Google." That is their title tag right there. Immediately below the hyperlink containing the title is the description that says, "Advertise with Google ad words, next to Google search results to boost website traffic and sales." That wording is within the <description> </description> tag on their website. By entering a title tag and a description tag -- which you will do in Word Press and it's easy to do --you're making the decision on what Google is going to show people about your website in their search results. It's your chance to tell the world what you want them to know. **Make sure your target keyword is in your description tag.**

In green in each Google search engine result is the URL (not a hyperlink). If you have an exact match domain, have your main keyword in the title tag, and your main keyword in the description tag, that's the search engine display "triple crown," to use a sports analogy. You are out of the gate ahead of everyone else for that keyword, and if you do what we tell you in this book and don't make any big mistakes, you have an outstanding shot at finishing number one.

When you think of a certain niche or product, there are certain websites you think of immediately. Those are the authority websites, and Google gives them higher search rankings, generally speaking, because they are websites that people frequently want to see. And, these are sites that other websites link to a lot. They have a lot of content that people are liking.

Some authority websites include Google, Yahoo,

Facebook, YouTube, and thousands more that have become go-to sites in their respective niches. Google's gives authority sites higher rankings, all things being equal, than competitors, because of their obvious popularity. For example, Facebook is an authority site. One trick is to set up a Facebook fan page with your EMD as the name, if it's available from Facebook as a custom URL. With very little work, you can realize high rankings from that page. I have numerous Facebook pages ranking number one overall for specific EMD searches, and many more on the first page of Google.

Facebook pages have limitations, however. Despite what it may seem, not everyone has a Facebook account. People who don't have a Facebook account can't view Facebook pages. Plus, Facebook does not give you complete freedom in the way you want to display your content. Even so, you should get a Facebook custom URL for your EMD. My experience has been that they rise slowly to the top of the rankings with almost no SEO work required.

We bring up authority sites primarily because it's important when you're looking at your competition for a keyword search in Google to ask, "Who's ahead of me?" It's a much, much more difficult road to climb if you have one or more authority websites ahead of you, as opposed to non-authority websites. Keep that in mind as you're doing your research on how you're going to proceed.

If you see that most of page 1 for a specific search is full of sites like YouTube, Facebook, Wikipedia and

CNN, just know that you face a massive job in jumping over sites like that. Sometimes the smartest course of action is to find a related keyword term that doesn't have Internet titans blocking your path to the top.

It's also a plus when you place an outbound link to an authority site in your topic or niche on a page you're trying to rank. Google's bots perceive that as adding value for your readers, so there is some ranking benefit to be realized by doing this.

We listed the key elements that need to be on the page you want to get ranked. You might be surprised about what doesn't need to be there. It used to be that you had to have an article of some sort on a page for it to have a chance to rank. Google doesn't tell you this, but we have found in our research that it just doesn't matter anymore whether you have an article or not. Many past SEO programs have involved writing lots of articles and having lots of articles outsourced. You don't need to do that anymore.

CHAPTER REVIEW

The must-haves on your page are:

- Analytics
- Headline/title including your target keyword phrase with H1 tag
- YouTube video
- Outbound link to "authority" website
- Interior link to a page in silo sequence

- Title tag including your target keyword
- Description tag including your target keyword

If you don't already have some other reliable page creation platform that you are confident with, go with WordPress. And don't forget to get a Facebook custom URL for your EMD.

5 LINK BUILDING DO'S AND DON'TS

All of the previous material covered here notwithstanding, we are finding that linkbuilding with PR links is the most reliable method to give your site or page a bump in the search engine rankings. You MUST have all of the previously covered elements in place to reach your highest potential.

We return to the farm and our silo to map out this ultra-important step in SEO. Remember our silo structure:

Best prices

After you have done your keyword research, purchased your domain, and set up your site with the elements laid out in the previous chapter, you are ready to test the viability of this project. We're going to test whether this page we have created has the potential for high rankings. This is particularly important if you don't have an exact match domain (EMD).

We mentioned that PR backlinks are very powerful in boosting your site's ranking. You may have been wondering, just how do I get someone with a PR page to link back to me. You may have guessed: you pay them.

There are several websites that broker this service – basically serving as the facilitator to match up people like us who need a PR backlink, and the people who have PR-ranked sites who are willing to sell backlinks. We use backlinks.com for this service.

For the test, you will need to purchase a PR 3 or greater backlink to the page that is the top page INSIDE your silo. Make sure that you're purchasing from a site that is in a similar content niche. A PR 3 link will cost somewhere between $20 or $30. The charge is an ongoing monthly charge through Paypal, and you may want to keep it in place if it has brought your site great results. But if you are using the backlink for testing purposes only, you can cancel your subscription payment through Paypal after a couple of weeks if you wish.

It's critical that your backlink "anchor text" include your targeted keyword phrase from your top-of-the-silo page. Most text hyperlinks have a blue line underneath, or some other visual cue that it's a hyperlink. The text that is in that link is called the anchor text and that's important.

Let's just say we're talking about the apartments again. If we have a page that is the apartments in Beavercreek Ohio, and it links out to our apartments in Los Angeles page with an anchor text link that says "apartments in Los Angeles," that is an indicator of a quality link for Google's bots because there is some contextual relationship in the content of the two pages. If we have a page about molten lava that links out to a page about apartments, that backlink is not given as much quality by Google, because there is no apparent contextual connection between the two pages.

While you can check Google to find out where your new page is ranking, chances are good that a new page won't show up in the top few search results pages for some period of time. It's a good idea to find an application that will track the rankings of your site over time for certain keywords. We recommend advancedwebranking.com.

A few days after you've purchased your test PR link, check back on the rankings of your page for the keyword. If the page has jumped to page 2 or 3 on Google, that's an indication that you have a shot at page-one ranking with additional work. At this point, if you have set everything up as outlined earlier here, it's all about additional link-building.

Your link-building MUST appear to Google as though it is occurring organically – through the natural course of humans seeing, liking and linking to a page. You've certainly heard of the Google Penguin and Panda updates, which targeted sites that were obviously not linked organically. (This goes back to an early chapter in which we pointed out that Google does not endorse SEO, because it sees SEO as an unnatural manipulation of its product.)

So what are the characteristics of organic (or at least, organic-looking) link-building?

1. Links must come from a wide variety of different IP addresses

Each computer on the internet has its own digital address that usually has 3 digits.3 digits.3 digits.3 digits. An example would be 123.456.789.123. Google looks for backlinks that come from as many different IP addresses as possible. If there are 100 backlinks to a site and 90 of them come from the same IP, what Google's bots are going to deduce is there's just one person or company that's sending all these links and they're trying to fake it. They're not really truly linking because they like it. They're sending a bunch of links there because they're trying to SEO and game the system.

2. Varied anchor text.

Remember how important it is for your backlink's anchor text to contain the targeted keyword phrase? SEO practitioners have known that for quite awhile, and one result was that some sites that were obviously SEO'd had a huge percentage of backlinks with the identical anchor text. That is a dead giveaway to Google, so you have to have anchor text variety.

Earlier in this book we mentioned a software product called SENuke. What this product will do is build a backlink profile from different IP addresses and with varied anchor text automatically. You have to set up the parameters for the campaign so the software knows what to do. What this achieves is what we call the backlink foundation.

While the backlink foundation does not, in and of itself, boost your rankings significantly, it sends signals to Google that the linkbuilding that is occurring is organic instead of contrived.

That, in turn, allows the PR backlinks that you purchase to have the intended effect while significantly reducing the chances of any penalization by Google.

SENuke is not the only software service that allows you to build a backlink foundation, but it's the one we use. If you have enough time in the day, or if you can outsource the work to someone, you can build thousands of backlinks to a site. When you start to reach that quantity of backlinks that appear organic, Google takes notice and your rankings increase because of the perceived popularity of the site.

CHAPTER REVIEW

Proper backlinking procedure is:

- Purchase a test backlink from a PR 3 site to see if it moves the page at the top of your silo to at least page 2 or 3 of Google. Give it a few days before you make any final judgments.
- If your page jumps to Google page 2 or 3, then it's time to really go to work. The best way to build a backlink foundation is through SENuke or other similar backlink building software.
- When you have a backlink foundation in place, you can add additional PR links with exact-match anchor text to have the maximum effect.

If you do it right, you can have great success. If you do it incorrectly you can really get yourself in trouble -- not legally, but with Google.

6 HOW TO ASSESS YOUR COMPETITION

An important aspect of keyword research is assessing your competition. We addressed the impact that authority sites have on Google rankings, but don't assume that just because you don't see any authority sites atop the rankings for your chosen keywords, that it's going to be a walk in the park.

There are hundreds of thousands, if not millions, of people who are doing the same thing you are trying to do – get top rankings. It's very possible, if not likely, that the sites you see atop Google for your keyword got there through conscious SEO.

What this chapter is all about is to give you a way to assess just how much SEO was needed to get to the top of the rankings for your chosen keyword, and whether trying to duplicate it is something you want to attempt. Some will be relatively simple. Some will be hugely difficult and time-consuming. It's better to know what you're up against before you start to compete.

We'll be addressing the off-page factors here. The presumption is that you have done all of the on-page optimization possible to put yourself in a position to be able to achieve top rankings.

"I'll use the (Google AdWords) keyword planner to uncover my primary keyword that I want to rank for," said Brett Combs, my partner in PropellerHead SEO. "Often times if I am doing this work for a client, I really already know what that keyword is because they've established that with me. But what I'm going to do is still go out and use the (keyword) planner to do basic research."

"... The thing that it lets me do is it lets me see what the related keywords are and how those keywords are generating traffic, because I want to keep all that in mind when I start to do the competitive analysis of competitor sites."

Start with an exact match keyword. Go to Google, enter the keyword with quotation marks around it. Doing the search with quotation marks will cut down the number of competing web pages to give you more of a true reflection of who you're competing against in that specific keyword phrase. Most likely, the person that's actually doing the searching is not using this because it's not a technique that's well known. But we use it for optimization to see who our true competitors are.

In the list of "true competitors" that Google produces

from that search with quotation marks, the first thing you want to do is see if there are a lot of authority sites -- like Wikipedia, WebMD, YouTube – in the top 10.

If you've got all top 10 sites that are all authority sites, you're going to have a very difficult time muscling that keyword up on the first page. Just putting your eyeballs on an exact match search results page will reveal a lot.

The following example was done in early September 2013. Search engine rankings change over time, so if you attempt to recreate the following example, it's likely to be different. But the points about the mindset and process of analyzing your SEO competitors remain valid.

We decided to check for potential competition in the keyword, women's hats. Going to Google and entering "women's hats" produced 857,000 results.

Looking through the results, the page was full of authority sites -- Nordstrom, Overstock, Macy's and many others that you might expect to show up for that search.

It's only necessary to assess the first page of results, because so few people click over to page two of results that it really doesn't matter if you are on page two.

Right smack in the middle of all of those authority sites, there are two that are not so-called authority sites, and there is a possibility that we might be able to outrank them. (Note: This is in no way a reflection of the quality of the content on the two websites in question. It is merely a reflection of the "authority" influence of the domain names as compared to the shopping titans surrounding them. The fact that they show up on the first page for this search is a tribute to the SEO work done on those sites.)

Both of the possible target sites have the phrase women's hats in the URL, and that's very important. That's called an in-URL use of the keyword. You'll see the instances of the words women's and hats, as well as the phrase women's hats in bold face type in Google.

"Google literally reveals to us what they're indexing and using to show this search," Combs said. "They're keying off hats, and they're keying off women's hats, and in the body text of the article, they're again keying off the exact match women's hats. That's what's probably causing the (high ranking) is that keyword right there is being used exactly that way."

The next step is to copy the URL and visit MajesticSEO.com. It's one of the most powerful websites for SEO. If you're able to start to dig through the metrics that it is tracking and you combine that with some other metrics from other websites, you're able to see what they are doing to help them achieve the rankings.

Keep in mind, however, that MajesticSEO measures only the off-page optimization carries more weight in Google's eyes than on-page optimization.

You can have the prettiest website and most well-optimized website, best articles written and all of that and we'll still never make it to Google on the top 10 with all of that because we hadn't taken care of the more important factor, which is the off-page optimization.

At MajesticSEO.com, paste in the URL of the site you want to learn more about, and select the "fresh index" option. On the date we looked at this, there was an indication on the MajesticSEO page that they had crawled 536 billion pages – a huge database that an SEO (search engine optimizer) can play around in to gain insight on what a competitor is doing.

In MajesticSEO, Combs entered one of the two targeted women's-hats URLs.

"This is revealing, and it's actually exciting because I think we could actually rank for this keyword. And let's talk about what are some things that we want to look at here to give us a clue on how we might go about ranking for that keyword," he said.

The summary tab in MajesticSEO showed that the web page in question had 47 external backlinks from 13 referring domains, coming from 12 IPs and 12 subnets. Forty-seven backlinks is not all that many in SEO terms. (Subnets means that they're on different class C IPs.)

An IP address has 4 octets, and the octets from which the backlinks are coming are almost all different. This is good in Google's eyes.

If you have a ton of backlinks that are all coming from a small number of IPs, that indicates to Google that the backlinking is being done artificially instead of naturally by people all over the web reacting to good content.

If you pay money to Majestic SEO, you can literally look at that backlink profile on a cumulative or noncumulative view and see what the history is for it. (Note: You do not need a paid membership to use MajesticSEO's basic functionality.)

Another MajesticSEO metric to check is the link profile. Anything that has a citation flow of 10 or greater or a trust flow of 10 or greater is a good website. Anything that's less than 10 on either one of those is either a struggling website, a new website, or a website that has had poor optimization done on it.

You can get the definition of what each MajesticSEO metric is by clicking on the little help icon on each one. Citation flow, for example, is a weighted citation given to a URL or domain. You'll see a citation flow graph. The best looking graph would have points grouped in a way where there are not too many outliers that are outside that line that is oriented at a 45-degree angle.

The women's-hats-related URL we pasted into MajesticSEO had 47 backlinks from 13 different domains from 12 different Class C IPs. Those numbers offer a guide as to what needs to be done to match and then eclipse that site.

A page with a higher number of backlinks does not necessarily make it something to avoid. We're going to try to create a similar set of high quality backlinks that are related to the business that we're trying to rank for or the content we're trying to rank for. We're going to try and match that to the best of our ability. So if that number is 1,000, that just means that it's going to take a little bit longer for us to fully implement our backlink program.

You can't go out and just blast out a thousand backlinks and expect Google not to pay attention and negatively impact your rankings. It's not a natural thing. It doesn't normally happen out in the real world through normal ways that people comment and post and refer to the site that's trying to rank. So if you go out and jam this, you're going to get in trouble.

Since the number of backlinks that need to be generated in this case would be relatively low, one approach to the off-page optimization would be to create a drip-feed campaign that will slowly drip those out and get your site ranked over time.

To get an idea of the kinds of links needed to match or eclipse your competitor, you can use Majestic SEO to analyze some of the top backlinks coming through the site that helped create that positive citation flow and trust flow by clicking the backlinks tab. (To do that, you will need to create an account and be logged in.)

The links displayed will be the ones that have the best flow metrics.

"What's so cool about this particular rank is that we literally could go and look at each one of these (backlinking) pages and just with our own eye and common sense, ask a very simple question: What are they doing that's creating that trust flow and creating a quality back link to the website?" Combs said. "It could be the page rank of the website, it could be the page rank of the referring back link, it could be the way they have the anchor text formatted, it could be article on the page -- there's a lot of factors that then turn into on-page factors on the outbound link."

From an SEO perspective, all we're doing is looking at what their anchor text is and then looking at the websites to see if any of them are authority sites, and really none of them are. They're all blogs or other shops. So once again, it helps bolster the case that we can go out and out-SEO this particular website because there's nothing on here that is an authority site.

So, the initial plan here would be to generate 47 backlinks from existing content on Google.

You literally can look at the backlinks that are getting your competitor's page ranked by going to the backlinks tab and looking at those websites, and see if there's any way that you can muscle a link in on those pages. Any backlink that comes from a blog gives an opportunity for another backlink through the commenting features available on most blogs.

Another option is to create a very simple website, using an expired domain that has page rank, to create a powerful backlink to the site you are trying to get ranked. You can go to one of the many services that broker these expiring domains (we recommend PRPowershot.com) and find a domain with page rank that contains the word hats (or if you are exceptionally lucky, there might be a domain with the phrase women's hats available).

In the case of this particular example, the backlink from the blog was from a PR 2 site, so you would ideally want to find at least a PR 2 domain to match the competing backlink, or PR 3 or higher to better it.

Since this is a pretty big keyword that generates a lot of traffic, you would want to spend the time and the money to set up a network of blogs that are on different Class C IPs -- a small network probably no more than 10. It's important to vary the anchor text of the backlinks from the various sites, in response to Google's recent changes that targeted some forms of SEO.

People were over-optimizing on the anchor tags by using the keywords that they wanted to rank for. Now you have to really "deoptimize" and only use that exact match a certain percentage of the time -- 10 or 20 percent, maybe less."

Once the 10 PR sites are built, they will be optimized using all of the techniques previously covered in this book.

"We'd send a small stream of backlinks to each of those 10 sites -- not to our money site, because we want to protect that at all costs," Combs said. "I mean that's just suicide (to send a backlink campaign directly at the site to be ranked). So what we're going to do is we're going to send those optimized anchor text backlink campaigns over a broad spectrum of web properties. We're going to send that to our 10 'pillow' sites, and then what will happen is over a period of time, could be days could be weeks, Google will index those links and transfer the page ranks to our money site and we should be able to outrank this hat site."

7 YOUR SECRET WEAPON: YOUTUBE VIDEOS

We have established in earlier chapters that "authority sites" such as Wikipedia, WebMD and others that have risen to the top of their niches due to the amount of information on them are going to top the rankings in Google, all things being equal.

Through months of testing, we established that your best chance of getting your content ranked – other than an exact match domain – is through YouTube video. You almost certainly have noticed that YouTube videos show up prominently in almost any Google search.

Not only is it possible to get ranked highly with YouTube videos, but you can actually rank multiple videos at or near the top of the first page.

If you can't get an exact-match domain, you can – using the techniques outlined in this chapter – move yourself at or near the top of the rankings in YouTube search (the second-largest search engine), and in some cases Google search.

As mentioned earlier, there is no more important aspect to SEO than keyword research, and that is the case in your quest to rank YouTube videos, as well. You want to find a keyword term or terms that get enough monthly searches to make the effort to rank worth your time and effort, while at the same time is not glutted with so many competitors that even a perfectly optimized video would face an uphill battle.

We recommend doing your keyword search in the AdWords Keyword Planner to find your target keywords, and then go to YouTube search and try searching for each of your targets with quotations " " around the keyword phrase. This will give you an idea of how many videos are optimized (either intentionally or unintentionally) for that exact-match phrase. With the techniques we will outline here, you stand a great chance for success if you can find keyword searches in quotations that have between 5,000 and 7,500 or fewer competing videos. You stand a chance on searches in quotations that show around 20,000 exact-match competitors. With numbers higher than that, your chances diminish just due to the number of competitors.

We'll show you exactly what you need to do for your "on-page" optimization. What you can't control or anticipate is the degree or extent of off-page optimization your competitors have done. However, you can use MajesticSEO.com to get an idea as a further step of your keyword research.

NAME YOUR VIDEO FILE

Once you have completed your keyword research, you should have a list of terms that you're targeting. We're presuming at this point that you have recorded your video and have it ready to upload to your YouTube account.

The video file you recorded probably has a name something like UEL83899.mp4 or .flv or .mov. The suffix does not matter, because YouTube can accept almost any file type. But the file name before the suffix (in this case, UEL83899) needs to be changed to the EXACT name you will give your video in the YouTube description. This is why you need to have your research done before uploading to YouTube.

We used this strategy to gain significant positioning in both YouTube and Google for the October 2013 launch of the Blog Beast mobile blogging product, for which we have an affiliate account.

We created several videos about this product, and used several of the keywords we had taken note of during a July 2013 convention in Denver where the upcoming product launch and release was announced. In Denver, the product was announced as "ENv2," short for Empower Network version 2. We did a lot of optimization of our blogs and websites for those terms and showed very good rankings for the identified terms. (See the screenshot of our rankings results in Google, Yahoo and Bing on the next page.)

What you'll see there is the rankings information

generated by the rankings tracker I used, called Rankerizer on Sept. 29, 2013. The ranking domain that you see, http://empowernetwork.com/eobsbiz, is my Empower Network blog used due to its status as an authority domain.

Domain: empowernetwork.com

Latest Full Update: September 29, 20 (about 10 hours ago)

Keyword	Google	Yahoo	Bing	Ranking URL (Domain or Page)
Empower Network sales engine	1	1	1	http://www.empowernetwork.com/eobsbiz/...
Empower Network version 2 average monthly earnings	1	-	1	http://www.empowernetwork.com/eobsbiz/...
Empower Network version 2 average earnings	2	1	1	http://www.empowernetwork.com/eobsbiz/...
Empower Network version 2 average weekly earnings	1	1	1	http://www.empowernetwork.com/eobsbiz/...
Empower Network version 2 launch date	6	3	3	http://www.empowernetwork.com/eobsbiz/...
Empower Network version 2 mobile audio-video broadcasting app	1	1	1	http://www.empowernetwork.com/eobsbiz/...
Get the Empower Network Version 2 app here	2	1	1	http://www.empowernetwork.com/eobsbiz/...
Empower Network version 2 mobile video app	2	3	3	http://www.empowernetwork.com/eobsbiz/...
Empower Network version 2 mobile video broadcasting app	1	4	4	http://www.empowernetwork.com/eobsbiz/...
Empower Network version 2 simple 2-click blogging platform	8	1	1	http://www.empowernetwork.com/eobsbiz/...
Empower Network version 2 simple blogging platform	4	1	1	http://www.empowernetwork.com/eobsbiz/...
ENv2 average monthly earnings	1	2	2	http://www.empowernetwork.com/eobsbiz/...
ENv2 average weekly earnings	1	3	3	http://www.empowernetwork.com/eobsbiz/...
ENv2 mobile audio-video broadcasting app	1	7	8	http://www.empowernetwork.com/eobsbiz/...
ENv2 mobile video app	1	9	9	http://www.empowernetwork.com/eobsbiz/...
ENv2 mobile video broadcasting app	1	3	3	http://www.empowernetwork.com/eobsbiz/...
ENv2 sales conversion engine	1	2	2	http://www.empowernetwork.com/eobsbiz/...
ENv2 sales	4	-	-	http://www.empowernetwork.com/eobsbiz/...
ENv2 sales engine	2	2	2	http://www.empowernetwork.com/eobsbiz/...
ENv2 simple blogging platform	2	4	3	http://www.empowernetwork.com/eobsbiz/...
ENv2 app	4	-	14	http://www.empowernetwork.com/eobsbiz/...
Get the ENv2 app here	1	2	2	http://www.empowernetwork.com/eobsbiz/...

You probably notice the keywords have the pattern to them that we described in the chapter about creating silos. That's why many of them are long-tail keywords.

Keep in mind that at the time this book was written, Empower Network had about 30,000 active affiliates. So these results were anything but gimmes. There was lots of competition for these keywords.

But then an interesting thing happened in early September. Empower Network issued a press release which referred to the product as "Blog Beast" instead of "ENv2." It was obvious they had realized the same thing I realized when doing keyword research – there is already a mobile phone product known as ENv2.

From my perspective as an SEO practitioner, that was a very difficult ranking challenge. From the Empower Network's perspective, it posed a branding challenge. I was glad they made the decision they made.

There was very little competition in Google and YouTube for the tern Blog Beast, along with the associated longer-tail keywords. So I created new videos that referred to Blog Beast, and named them these names, among others:

Viral blogging system: Blog Beast!
Blog Beast: New viral blogging system doubling as viral marketing platform
Blog Beast mobile app: INSTANT video and audio blogging!

You want the name to be keyword-rich without being obviously keyword-stuffed – more for the benefit of the person doing the search seeking information on your keyword. Would you be more likely to click on one of the video titles above, or one that was "Blog Beast Blog Beast Blog Beast Blog Beast"? The latter will probably rank very highly, but will send the immediate message of "spam" to the person who is scanning the results of a search in the blink of an eye and deciding upon which one he or she will click.

Tip: Put your primary keyword first. In the bullet-pointed examples above, the first one "Viral blogging system: Blog Beast!" should have had the phrase "Blog Beast" first, followed by the phrase "viral blogging system." But an unintended consequence of that juxtaposition is that that particular video was ranking number four overall in YouTube for the search "viral blogging system," in early October 2013, and climbing.

Now, returning to your video file: UEL83899.mp4. Rename it to the exact title you are giving the video in YouTube description. In this case, using the examples above, the file would be named blog-beast-new-viral-blogging-system-doubling-as-viral-marketing-platform.mp4. (Note: I have not tested whether the results are better, worse or the same if you don't put hyphens between the words. That's my standard style and it is working so far.)

Once you have renamed the file, upload it to YouTube.

ON-PAGE OPTIMIZATION

You can do this as your video is uploading to YouTube. In the title field, put the exact same title as you did when you named the video, minus the hyphens.

Believe it or not, this is 80 percent of the battle. Where you now have to outduel your competitors is in the aspects of on-page YouTube optimization that the vast majority of them don't know, such as renaming the video file before uploading, and the following:

In the description field, copy the title from the title field and paste it in at the beginning of the description field. Immediately after that, type in the URL you want people to ultimately click on to see your page or offer. You want that to be very high in the description, because YouTube displays the first 140 or so characters of your video description in the search results, and URLs are clickable hyperlinks. Just make sure you put http:// before the domain name so the URL becomes clickable.

What I did next is I pasted the text of the scripts I submitted to the people from fiverr.com who did the voiceovers for me on the videos. If you don't have that, a description that you write about the video will be fine.

Tags: Make sure all of your keywords are included in the tags.

Thumbnails: When the video is done uploading and rendering, you will have the choice of three different thumbnail images. Make sure you choose one that is interesting, visually bright and vibrant. Your YouTube account may provide you the option to upload a custom thumbnail, and I would certainly recommend that if none of the thumbnail images generated from your video file are bright and attention-getting. (This will depend on the status of your YouTube account and how many subscribers you have, whether this option is available to you.) Once your video is ranked highly, it then has to vie for attention among a dozen or so others, and you will find that most of them have custom thumbnails. It is a well-known fact of advertising and marketing that you have to grab the viewer's attention. Don't miss this opportunity to do so, because your competitors aren't.

OFF-PAGE OPTIMIZATION

These factors aren't as critical in YouTube and Google's eyes, but you have to assume that most of your serious competitors are doing them to get every edge they possibly can. There is some expense related to these, and your budget and willingness to dip into it will affect how far you can take them.

First, go to Fiverr.com and create an account there, if you don't already have one. If you don't know what Fiverr.com is, it is a place you can get almost any task – online or otherwise – completed for a fee starting at $5. (Most vendors have upsells to higher levels of service.)

At Fiverr.com, do a search for "YouTube high retention views." What you will get is a list of contractors who will, for $5 or more, provide a specified number of views on your YouTube video. More views equals more interest in the eyes of YouTube, and this usually means higher rankings.

High retention is important. YouTube and Google have started giving more favor to videos that people watch for a substantial portion of the video. If the views are not high-retention, they will have less impact than a similar number of views that are. Our experience has shown that high-retention is very important.

Then, using the techniques described earlier in this book, create a campaign of high PR backlinks to your YouTube video URL.

MULTIPLE VIDEOS

If you really want to carve out some digital real estate in YouTube search, make several videos and follow the same process with each of them.

If you have one video that you really like, and would like to leverage it for ranking for several keywords, you will need to alter that video in some way before you upload it to YouTube again, because YouTube rejects duplicate uploads. (Note: Changing the name of the video is not enough. You actually need to go in and add, subtract or edit existing content in the video, and then save a new version.)

There are many free options for video editing, including Windows Movie Maker that comes with most Windows machines, and iMovie that comes with most Apple machines. I personally recommend Camtasia studio if you are someone who has more than a novice level of expertise at video editing. Camtasia Studio 8, the most recent version, has added green screen (chromakey) functions, which I have used extensively in the videos I created for the campaign described above.

Here are some screenshots of results we achieved in YouTube search within a relatively short period of time. (Screenshots taken on October 5, 2013; all showing top of first page results.)

Keyword: **Blog Beast** (see screenshot, next page)

By the time you are reading this, these rankings will very likely have changed. But in terms of strategy, it would have been difficult to do much better than this at the time.

The Blog Beast launch was going to happen beginning on October 7, in two days. So, for people who did the search for Blog Beast in YouTube, there was an 80 percent chance if they clicked on one of the top five videos, it would be one of mine.

Whether they convert into sales is a separate issue which I will learn. But from an SEO perspective, this is ideal. What you can't see in the screenshot is two more of my videos further down on the first page.

Keyword: **Blog Beast app**

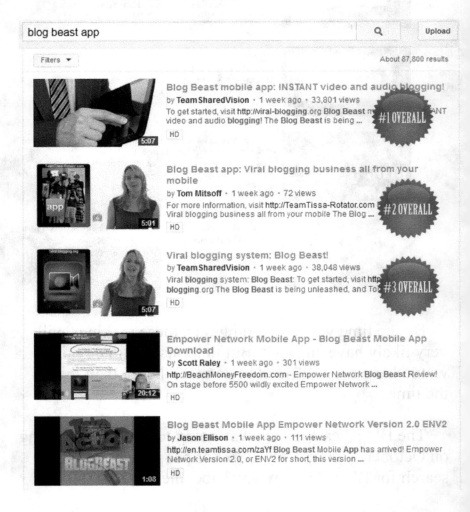

They always say that the gold is in the top three, and we had that covered leading into the product launch, along with one more further down the page that wasn't captured in the screenshot.

Keyword: **Blog Beast movie**

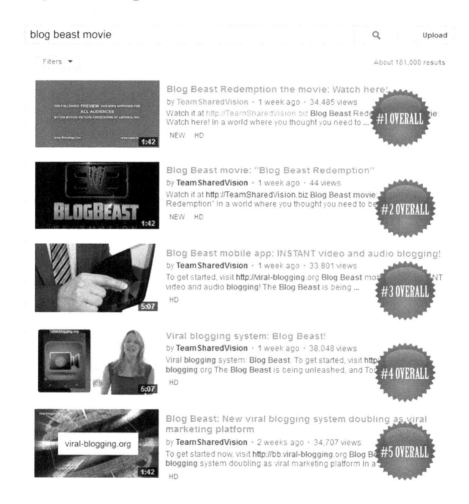

You'll note that the video in the number two position has the exact phrase "Blog Beast movie" in the title, and it was optimized for that phrase. At the time we were writing this chapter, we were testing to see how it would fare without the extra YouTube views purchased through Fiverr. Interestingly, you can see that the only video ahead of it has the three words (Blog, Beast, movie) in the title (but not in exact match sequence), and also has the additional views. You can see that by virtue of the optimization for the name, that #2 video outranks other videos that are not optimized for Blog Beast movie but have tens of thousands of views. That goes to illustrate and reinforce the importance of exact-matching your keyword in your title and description as mentioned earlier.

Chalk at least part of this success story up to a bit of speculative YouTube search real estate squatting. Part of the Blog Beast launch was a series of videos that Empower is promoting as having been produced on an actual movie set. So this was set up in case the "Blog Beast movie" gets a lot of buzz and subsequent searches. It's an effort that could either pay off big time or produce a big zero. That's part of being an entrepreneur – being willing to take a chance and investing some time and money in something that is anything but a sure thing.

The Blog Beast keyword search focus applied to one very specific company and product. Part of the success of this effort will come by being able to reach people who are not searching for the specific product name, but still looking for the results the product can provide. So ...

Viral blogging: #5, #6, #10, #17 overall;
Viral blogging system: #5, #8, #11;

Viral blogging platform: #2, #6
Mobile blogging: #4
Mobile blogging system: #2, #4, #6, #8
Mobile blogging platform: #10, #14

On October 5, 2013, those were the results for our videos in YouTube searches on those secondary keywords that we identified as part of the keyword research and used in some video names, but have not focused a campaign directly on those keywords. You will get lots of rankings you don't expect when you optimize your videos as we have described in this chapter.

Oh, did we forget to mention Google?

Even though YouTube is owned by Google, the ranking algorithms for the two are not identical. The exact-match of the keyword in the title and description is much, much more important in YouTube than in Google. The off-page factors are much more important in Google than YouTube.

But one thing is clear to anyone who uses Google to any extent: YouTube videos are occupying more and more of a percentage of real estate in Google search, and they are outranking most non-video websites and web pages. You can attribute this in part to the fact that there are millions of YouTube videos produced every day, so it makes sense that there would be more showing up in search. You also have to acknowledge that Google's ownership of YouTube is very likely a factor in YouTube videos being given high priority in the ranking algorithm.

CHAPTER RECAP

Unless you have an authority domain, your best chance of ranking highly in competitive keyword searches is through a YouTube video campaign that directs viewers to your website or affiliate link.

As you embark on this track, it is important to ALWAYS keep in mind that your video content is not in your control once you upload it to YouTube.

When I uploaded the videos mentioned in this chapter, I was one of the first, if not the first, there for the Blog Beast and related keywords. One unexpected consequence of that is that people looked at the videos, thought they were good, and then downloaded them from YouTube and turned around and uploaded them to their own accounts with their own affiliate links. Unless you have an attorney and are willing to spend some money on legal action, there is not a lot you can do about this, except …

Brand the heck out of your videos. Using Camtasia Studio 8, I have added my Team Shared Vision business logo and a website URL to each video. So now, if someone is going to take it without permission, they are going to have to weigh what it means having my logo and my URL in a video that they are using to try to get someone to click to their offer.

And also, don't forget that YouTube controls your channel, not you. Your channel can be shut down with no notice and with no recourse. You should always keep an archive of all of your videos in the event YouTube shuts you down. While not likely, it's happened to people who I know. You have to weigh the undeniable SEO benefits of YouTube with the control you lose over your own content.

When brainstorming one of these YouTube ranking campaigns, you should be thinking short-term. Get your videos in place for a product launch or event, and then ride them for a few weeks or months.

The exception to this would be for local rankings or very low-competition keywords, for which an onslaught of competitors across the country or globe is unlikely. The methods described in this chapter can provide excellent long-term rankings for videos in searches that have a lower level of competition.

8 YOU'RE READY

Well, you're ready to get started! This manual has provided you with everything you need to get started on excellent search engine ranking results.

But maybe you have read this and thought, "Wow, I had no idea that there was so much to do. I can do it, but I don't have the time."

If that's you, we offer the services of PropellerHead SEO to you, as described throughout this manual. Just visit our website at http://propellerheadseo.com and look for the contact us tab.

And, if you are interested in learning more about the business opportunities available through my Team Shared Vision, please visit http://teamsharedvision.com.

If you want to be notified of big changes in SEO strategy – and they happen very often due to the nature of changes in Google and YouTube, visit the website for this manual at http://webrankingmanual.com, where you can sign up for e-mail notifications of changes that you need to know.

We will provide occasional video updates, as well, so just do a YouTube or Google search for Web Ranking Manual and subscribe to the video channel so you can receive updates automatically.

You are now ready to be found online!

ABOUT THE AUTHOR

Tom Mitsoff, an SEO and online business expert, specializes in maximizing the exposure businesses, companies, products and individuals can receive in search engines like Google, YouTube, Yahoo and Bing.

Tom is the founder and CEO of Expert Online Business Solutions (**http://eobs.biz**), Team Shared Vision (**http://teamsharedvision.com**), and a partner in Propellerhead, a Texas search engine optimization company serving companies of all sizes (**http://propellerheadseo.com**).